Next Level Dad

Bringing Faith and Fun to Fatherhood

By Derek L. Polen

Copyright © 2016 by Goal Line Group LLC

All rights reserved. No part of this publication may be reproduced, stored in a retrieval system, or transmitted by any means – electronic, mechanical, photographic (photocopying), recording, or otherwise – without prior permission in writing from the author.

Disclaimer: This book is presented solely for educational and entertainment purposes. This information is provided and sold with the knowledge that the author and publisher do not offer any legal or other professional advice. In the case of a need for any such expertise consult with the appropriate professional. This book should only serve as a general guide and not as the ultimate source of subject information. This book has not been created to be specific to any individual or organization's situation or needs. Every individual is different and the advice and strategies contained herein may not be suitable for your situation. The author and publisher make no representations or warranties of any kind and assume no liabilities of any kind with respect to the accuracy of the contents and specifically disclaim any implied warranties of merchantability or fitness of use for a particular purpose. The author and publisher shall have no liability or responsibility to any person or entity regarding any loss or damage incurred, or alleged to have incurred, directly or indirectly, by the information contained in this book. The author and publisher take no responsibility for the business practices or performance of any product or service of any of the mentioned companies in the book. Trademarked names are used in this book in an editorial context with no intention of infringement of that trademark.

ISBN-13: 978-1533134349   ISBN-10: 1533134340
Printed by Createspace, an Amazon.com Company

To my parents who taught me so much

Thanks to God for blessing me with
the opportunity to be a father

TABLE OF CONTENTS

Next Level Journey	1
The Reason for 40 Ways	5
God Driven	9
CFO (Chief Fun Officer)	35
Get in the Game	59
Every Day is a Classroom	73
Ready to Be a Next Level Dad?	103
A Prayer for You	109

Next Level Journey

I am truly blessed by God to be the Earthly father of the children he gave me. In Psalm 127:3 it says that children are "...a reward from him". Before children, my life revolved around my corporate career. Now, my kids are my focus and my priorities have shifted in a much better way.

Being a father truly is a blessing and a role not to be taken for granted. We are being given the opportunity to help influence the next generation and in this world we need more Godly leaders being developed. By our faith, and with the help of God, we can build the character of our children in a way that honors God and can move the world in the right direction.

I am still learning as a father and I always will be building more knowledge into my daddy database. I am not a perfect father either, but I work hard to be a good father and I strive to be a better father every day.

Throughout this book I will share with you 40 different ways I have incorporated into my role as a father. These ideas come from learnings growing up, what I have learned as a father today, and from the word of God. I make every effort to live by these ideas, so I can enhance my effectiveness as a father.

The ideas are grouped into 4 categories. With everything we do, it is important to put God first. Thus the first group is, "*God Driven*". These ideas come from what I have learned in church and through Bible study. The next group is, "*CFO (Chief Fun Officer)*". It is important that we be fun dads who make our kids laugh and use humor and excitement to teach them. The third group is, "*Get in the Game*". As a father it is easy to be consumed with careers and other responsibilities, but being involved in the lives of our children is very important. The last group is, "*Every Day is a Classroom*". This area gives us the opportunity to really teach and equip our children with skills and traits that will help them be successful in life.

Woven throughout the book there are meaningful Bible verses to reflect on. All of these ideas can effectively help you change the way you think about being a father and help you take your father role to the next level.

THE REASON FOR 40 WAYS

I developed 40 because of its biblical significance. In the Bible it represented times of testing that led to reward or fulfillment. And, what can be more testing and rewarding than raising kids!

Some 40 day Bible examples:

- It rained 40 days/nights causing the flood in Noah's story (Genesis 7:12)
- Moses was on Mount Sinai 40 days/ nights fasting while receiving the Ten Commandments (Exodus 34:28)
- Elijah's 40 day/night fasting and journey to the mountain of God (1 Kings 19:8)
- Jesus fasted for 40 days and 40 nights (Matthew 4:2)
- After Jesus' resurrection he was on Earth 40 days (Acts 1:3)

This simple guide has 40 ways to help you take being a father to another level through fun ideas, ways to get more involved, and to bring more faith-based principles into your father role. This 40 way approach is about respecting the significance of 40 from our biblical history and giving you many new ways or encouraging reminders on how we can be the best fathers we can be.

God Driven

1. Talk To God

Prayer is the most important thing you can do as a father. You may or may not be someone who prays regularly or even at all. If you do not pray at all, I hope you will start today because it is critically important.

Pray For Your Children
When I pray to God for my kids my prayers usually focus on three things. I pray for their safety, their health, and that my kids will make good decisions that please the Lord.

Pray With Your Children
I encourage you to pray <u>daily</u> with your kids. It is great to do it at breakfast, lunch, or dinner. I usually do it in the car or in the parking lot right before they go to school. It is a great way to start off their day. I pray for the same things as I mention above when I pray for them, but will also

take this time to pray for others and also thank God for all His blessings.

Pray For Your Kids School
During the school year our kids spend most of their days in the classroom. The school is where they learn most of their knowledge whether it is from teachers or from classmates. First pray that your children listen to the teachers, are in a safe environment, and make good choices while they are there; including surrounding themselves with the right kind of friends, ones who will be a positive influence. I also pray for their teachers to bring passion and creativity into the classroom, so that they teach effectively.

Pray For Yourself
When you pray to God regarding your needs, seek His guidance. Ask Him to help you be a better father and to help equip you with the wisdom to be the father that He wants you to be.

"Do not be anxious about anything, but in everything, by prayer and petition, with thanksgiving, present your requests to God."
– Philippians 4:6

2. Helping Hands

Serving others is one of the main biblical responsibilities we have. Since my children were in preschool, we have introduced them to serving at different non-profit events. They have helped with food drives, Thanksgiving meal preparations, and wrapped Christmas presents for children in need. These are fun and rewarding moments for them.

Last summer we really took it up a notch. Our summer was full of fun and adventure, but we made an effort to serve several times at a global missions organization. We would prepare care packages and sort clothes and shoes, which would be given to people in need. My kids learned ways to work as a team and use their abilities to help others.

When summer was complete, we reflected on our favorite memories of the summer. The kids agree that helping others in need was one of the main highlights of the summer. These service opportunities helped my kids learn how to work in teams, but most importantly appreciate the blessings they have. It does not take much time or any special skills to make a huge impact in someone else's life.

To find ways to serve together here are some suggestions on where to start searching:

- Church
- Ask a friend or co-worker
- Food pantry
- Schools
- Non-For-Profits that have a mission you are passionate about

"Each one should use whatever gift he has received to serve others, faithfully administering God's grace in its various forms."
— 1 Peter 4:10

3. Gracious Givers

Giving to others is one of the main responsibilities God requires us to do. You can give in many different ways. You can give your time, your finances, your knowledge, or any of your talents and abilities to help others. We all have good intentions and it is easy to set aside or forget, but we must make giving a priority.

Giving Your Time – As mentioned in "Helping Hands", you give your time to help others. Sure, it is nice to use your free time to watch television, hang out with friends, or work on a project, but allocate a little time each week to helping others. You can volunteer at a local mission group, serve at a food pantry, help with fundraising, or serve in a variety of other impactful ways.

Giving Your Finances – This is a tough one for many, but it can make such a huge impact. You first start with your tithes and from there try to donate more to others. God takes what we give and multiplies it for the benefit of others.

Giving Your Knowledge & Talents – This relates to giving your time by physical service, but takes it a step further and applies your mental know-how to help others. For example, maybe you are good at finances and you could lead a financial stewardship class at church, or you could become a mentor, maybe you like building things so you could help Habitat for Humanity or at a mission trip to build orphanages. The key is to identify areas of skills you know a lot about and figure out ways to apply your expertise in the service arena.

When you give together as a family, you are putting God first and other's needs first. You are making them the priority and using what you have been blessed with to help bless others.

"In everything I did, I showed you that by this kind of work we must help the weak, remembering the words the Lord Jesus himself said: 'It is more blessed to give than to receive.'" - Acts 20:35

4. 1st and 10

Throughout the Bible, we are instructed to tithe through verses that talk about giving our first fruits, honoring the Lord with our finances, and giving back a tenth of what we earn. When we tithe, we honor God, help the church, and help others. I do believe he blesses us in return.

Tithes that go to the church help it thrive. Sure, they have costs associated with personnel, utilities, insurance, materials, and more, but what the church does with the tithes is what is so rewarding to see. The church uses this money to reach unchurched people, help those in need, plant more churches, and bring more people into the kingdom of God.

So how does this play into being a dad? Well, for one it is an instruction from God and for us to help get our kids to do it, it starts with us. If you already tithe, great! If you do not, give it a chance. Another reason is so that we can get our children into the routine of tithing on a regular basis at an early age. Starting this at an early age gives another opportunity for them to put God first in another facet of their life, their finances.

"Honor the Lord with your wealth,
with the firstfruits of all your crops."
– Proverbs 3:9

5. Ask This Question

As much as we would like to think we know all the answers, we don't. Several years ago there was a popular acronym going around, "WWJD". It stood for "What Would Jesus Do?". That saying has always stuck in my head. It is very simple, yet an effective reminder for us to consider what would Jesus do in a situation.

Earlier I mentioned the importance of prayer, so to build on that we need to routinely seek God's guidance and ask ourselves; "What Would Jesus Do?". This applies virtually to anything we do. Consider what Jesus would do and try to approach it in a Christ-like manner.

We are not going to get it right every time, but if we study God's word and seek the help of God, then He can help us navigate through all of our parenting situations.

"Follow my example, as I follow the example of Christ."
– 1 Corinthians 11:1

6. Real Men Say "I Love You"

I remember when I was little, it would be 5:30am-6:00am, I would still be asleep, and I could feel my Dad's mustache tap my cheek as he kissed me before he went to work. Every day then, and still today, he (and my Mom) always tell me they love me after a phone call or when we visit.

Every morning, as my kids wake up I always try to either give them a kiss, hug, and/or tell them I love them. I also always give them a kiss and tell them I love them as they head to their classroom. At the end of the day I do the same. Honestly, I tell them I love them throughout the day.

You can never tell them you love them too much. It is important for them to hear you tell them and if you are lucky they will tell you they love you back (don't always count on that).

The words "I Love You", a kiss, or a hug, are the main things we associate with showing affection, but it does not stop with those. Just a simple conversation about how their day was, listening to them tell a story, giving them a smile, or just snuggling up on the couch together are just a few of many other ways to show them love. Tell them you love them often and show them how much they mean to you.

"Be imitators of God, therefore, as dearly loved children and live a life of love, just as Christ loved us and gave himself up for us..."
– Ephesians 5:1-2

7. Bigger Than Football Sunday

When children go to church at an early age they build the spiritual foundation they need in life. Attending church not only builds them spiritually, but it starts shaping their character. This helps them outside of church, by knowing how to show love and compassion, how to forgive, how to make better decisions, and it gives them a servant's heart.

I can still remember the day we took my daughter to church when she was one week old. My children have grown to love church, meet new friends, and to love Jesus even more. It saddens me when I have seen so many families attend church, minus the father. Usually because he has not accepted Christ into his heart and feels uncomfortable, or he wanted to sleep in, or because he had to work. If he had to work, it is hard to get around that, but one suggestion would be to look for a service time at your church that better accommodates. If that does not work, and the work schedule conflicts with church indefinitely then it may be time to find a different church that offers a time that better fits your schedule.

Your level of faithfulness is not measured by your attendance. I will admit that our family does not go to church every Sunday. Throughout the week we pray every day, I watch sermons online and read devotionals, we study the Bible together, and I try to live every day in as much of a Christ-like manner as I can.

"And we pray this in order that you may live a life worthy of the Lord and may please him in every way; bearing fruit in every good work, growing in the knowledge of God."

– Colossians 1:10

8. The Continuous Learner

A devotional is simply time spent together in bible study. There are many devotional resources such as, devotional books, apps, videos, online resources, or simply pull straight from the bible.

You do not have to be a pastor to do these with your kids. All you have to do is read the devotional and discuss it. Talk about the meaning of the lesson and discuss ways your family can incorporate the teachings into your daily lives.

I have a Life Application Bible and it is great because there are study notes below the verses. After we reflect on the verses we read, we talk about ways we can practice it in the future. Many of the verses have these additional notes below to help us understand the meaning in more modern day terms and how we can use the meaning in our lives.

"For everything that was written in the past was written to teach us, so that through endurance and the encouragement of the Scriptures we might have hope."

— Romans 15:4

9. Show Your Love For God

Do you love a sports team so much that your kids love that team too? Or, maybe it is a hobby you love. They see you practically worship this team or hobby and they grow to love it also. Take that passion and start demonstrating that love to God.

There are many ways to show our love for God. Praise Him out loud, pray to Him with your children, or display something that shows your love for Christ. You can also show your Godly love by serving and showing love to others.

When you show your love for God your kids see that. One of our goals is to be a Man of Faith, one whose actions are for God and show our love for Him. We may not always win our children over to our favorite sports team, but by displaying our passion for God we can win our children over to His team.

"Love the Lord your God with all your heart and with all your soul and with all your strength."
– Deuteronomy 6:5

CFO
(Chief Fun Officer)

I love having fun with my children. Yes, I act goofy at times, but to see them smile or hear them laugh is so worth it. It is easy for us to be too serious sometimes. We have so much going on in our heads, various demands on our life, and the pressures of work. We cannot let all these things keep us from having fun. I do have many serious moments with my kids, but most of the time I try to handle things with them in a fun-loving way.

I ask myself, "When my kids grow up, do I want them to remember me as a grump, too strict and serious, or a fun dad?" Of course, I want to be a fun dad. Being a fun dad does not mean I don't discipline and instruct when necessary. It does mean that when the opportunity arises, I choose to engage in a more light-hearted way. Being a fun type of dad can help get our kids excited, plus it can be an effective way to teach them.

Let's go over some ways to expand our role of family CFO (Chief Fun Officer).

10. Be Silly

I have to admit, I have done many silly things with my kids that I am glad others have not seen. It is so important for them to see you have a sense of humor and as a father one of the most precious things you will ever see and hear is the giggling of your children.

So what are ways to be silly? Here is a list of a few ideas we have had so much fun with:

- Make up new games to play with them
- Dress up in costumes. We mix up different ones to create "hybrid heroes".
- Make forts with blankets, tables, and chairs
- Build a cardboard spaceship or boat
- Have water balloon fights
- Monster tag (unleash that inner Frankenstein)
- Get flashlights and have a light show
- Karaoke or have a dance party

I think you get the picture now. There are limitless ways to incorporate your goofiness into something that makes the kids laugh. Words of advice: Stretch out first and be careful. I have pulled a muscle many times and crushed my foot one time being "silly".

There is no perfect guide book on how to be silly. You do not have to be a standup comedian to make your kids laugh. The point is to just let loose and have a little fun with them. Set the demands of life aside for a moment and be a goofball with your kids. When you are making them laugh, I am sure you will be laughing too!

11. "Pop"arazzi

When God gave all of us our special gifts, mine was not in the photography department. I do not mind taking pictures, but I do not have that photographer's eye. The one thing I do have is a passion for capturing many of my children's moments.

When I titled this idea "Pop"arazzi, it refers to "Pop"=Dad and you merge that with paparazzi to get a major-photo-taking-Dad! With today's cell phones it is so much easier to take pictures everywhere we go.

An idea I started in 2014 was creating a picture book for my kids. It was titled the Summer of Adventures. Within the book were pictures of all the fun activities we did that summer. I gave each of my kids a copy of the book, so they could cherish as they got older. I made the hardcopy book online with one of the photo printing websites we use and it cost me about $20. You can do a regular photo album, but the online-created book allows you to add backgrounds, captions, and titles more easily.

Our children grow so quickly and we need to capture the moments as they grow. With today's technology it is easy to download the pictures to a computer, but you may forget pictures or you can lose them if your computer crashes. If you are good about printing them, then they could get lost in the picture abyss. Take it a step further and put the pictures into a book so that you can relive those special times with your children.

12. Be A Storyteller

Have you ever told your children a make believe story and you see their eyes all big as they listen fully engaged? Maybe you remember hearing them as a child from your parents or friends. Stories are like movies. A story can be full of adventure, have mystery, entertain, and inspire us.

There are two types of stories we can share with our children. There is the fictional story that we are all used to (ex: bedtime & campfire stories). The other type of story are factual life stories. I will share with them adventures I went on, sports stories, things I have seen, or places I have travelled.

These stories entertain which definitely makes it fun, but they can also teach and encourage them.

"Tell it to your children, and let your children tell it to their children, and their children to the next generation."

– Joel 1:3

13. Share Your Heritage

The older I get the more I want to learn about my heritage. The internet makes it easier to learn about our ancestors. I remember as a kid how cool it was to know I was part English and German, with supposedly a little Native American Indian, which I am still trying to confirm. As I researched my roots years later I have learned so much about family professions, military records, and other exciting stories (no royalty lineage found yet).

You do not have to be a historian by any means, but share your family's heritage with your kids. Share with them where their grandparents grew up, what relatives did for a living, any exciting stories you have about relatives, or traditions your family has had for generations. Sharing this knowledge with them helps them understand more of where they came from, and can help inspire them too!

14. Channel Your Inner Griswold

I love the old National Lampoon's Family Vacation movies with Chevy Chase playing Clark Griswold. Clark truly valued those big vacation trips with his family. I think my family would even say I display some of those Griswold characteristics myself…. fun, goofy, and all about creating the best family vacation experience.

For our family, our Wally World is Walt Disney World. It is our favorite place to visit as a family. My wife and I went a couple times before kids, but it was after we had kids when each trip became "magical". We can all ride the rides together, see great shows, and enjoy one-of-a-kind experiences. It is a place that has created so many great memories for my family.

Your Wally World can be someplace totally different. It could camping, hiking, and sleeping under the stars. Maybe it is going to a beach, or visiting a museum, or going to a sporting event, or something else.

When I say "Channel Your Inner Griswold", I mean plan for a new vacation experience for your family. Invest your time into the planning, research it together as a family, and build excitement before you go. We do not get much vacation time and with the time we get we have to make the most of it. When vacation time does come immerse yourself in it. Do not think about work, do not let anything bother you, and just be like Clark trying to create a memorable vacation experience for your family.

15. Write Them a Letter

What a great surprise to them if you could write them a letter. If you have trouble telling them in person how much they mean to you, then maybe a letter is a starting point (but it is no substitute). Put a note in their lunch box, put one by their bed before you go to work, or leave one before you go on a trip. Writing them little letters are a great way to encourage them and express your love to them.

I still have a couple letters my dad wrote me years ago. In the letters I write my kids, they are usually pretty simple. I tell them to have a good day, be safe, how proud I am of them, or some type of encouragement. In every letter I always tell them I love them.

16. Date Night or Guys Night

Ever since my daughter was little we would have a date night. We would go to any restaurant she wanted to eat at, go to a store and I would let her pick out something. We would also go do something fun like the movies or miniature golf.

We are fortunate at their school they have a Daddy & Daughter Dance. It is basically dads standing around a dance floor watching their daughters run around, but it is a very special night. You get a few slow dances with your daughter and a picture of the both of you all dressed up. Heads up, if you attend one of these, it is a preview of your dance with your daughter at her wedding and it may bring a tear to your eye.

Let's say you do not have a daughter and you have a son. You can still do these night outs with your buddy. I have these nights with my son and we will call them "Guys Night".

If you have more than one child, do these night outs with just one at a time. It gives them a chance to pick whatever they want to get or do. Plus they do not have to compete with a sibling for your attention. Let your child do most of the talking, and listen to them talk to you about school, friends, their interests, and enjoy this one-on-one time with your child.

17. Start Traditions

The older I get the more I appreciate the value of traditions. I am usually always on a quest to discover new traditions we can incorporate with our family. With traditions we all have memories of different ones we had with parents or a family member. Usually Christmas traditions are the ones that come to mind.

Every year at Christmas we build gingerbread houses, go out for hot chocolate and Christmas light looking, and sponsor buying gifts for children in need. A family favorite on Christmas Eve, we will attend church candlelight service, then go eat at a Chinese restaurant (kind of sounds like the movie, The Christmas Story), then when we arrive at home I will read from Luke 2 in the Bible.

Christmas is when we are used to doing traditional activities, but traditions can happen all throughout the year. There are traditions many of us have on holidays, birthdays, summer break, at the start of school year, and more. There are many opportunities to create those family traditions.

Chances are you already have some traditions with your family. I want to encourage you to look at how you could build upon existing traditions and also create new traditions you can do throughout the year. Traditions are important because they create special memories and are something for the family to look forward to year after year!

18. Tech Disconnect

When I was growing up I spent so much time outside. I would try and play basketball, football, or baseball every day of the year. If I was not playing sports I was riding my bike around town, swimming, or going on outdoor adventures. We did have computer (the great Commodore C64) and other game consoles, but yet I never planted myself in front of these machines or television like kids do today. The key was I was out being active and having fun.

Today we have so many more tech influenced sources. There are more TV programs, movies, smartphones, tablet devices, and game stations that capture the mindshare of our kids. Do not get me wrong, I love technology, but I think as a society we are letting it consume us. Technology is a great thing and creates so much entertainment. It also brings efficiencies into our lives, but too much for a kid can be bad since it hinders them from getting exercise and I personally feel it is effecting our communication skills.

In our house we do an occasional "No T.V. Tuesday" or we will say "Turn off the electronics, we're going outside". The kids may grumble at first, but they always enjoy what is to come. It always ends up being a peaceful, fun-filled time for our family.

When we are in the car we limit movie watching & tablet game playing to only long road trips. We have to remember that all these entertaining devices are not digital babysitters and it does not hurt for us to disconnect from them once in a while.

19. Experience Gifts

As a father I get so much enjoyment in buying my children gifts. I know some dads who hate shopping so much that they usually resort to one of three options: 1) let their spouse do the buying, 2) buy the biggest gift they can find to compensate for lack of knowing what the child really wants, or 3) they buy what is convenient. You do not have to love shopping, but we need to make some effort in our gift giving.

I buy my children their fair share of tangible gifts each celebratory event, but I have always been one who prefers to gift: Experiences. Experience gifts I have done in the past are professional ball games, tickets to a monster truck show, concerts, theatrical shows, or a trip out of town to do something fun. Granted these experiences may be more expensive, but I do not do them all the time.

The benefits of experience gifts are:

1) Creates a memory for your family that is more likely to be remembered than a physical gift.

2) Gives your kids something to look forward to.

3) Makes another opportunity for you and your child to spend more quality time together doing something fun.

20. Read To Them

I have to admit my wife is much better at this than I am. She is like Belle from Beauty & the Beast (guess that makes me the Beast). She spends a lot of time with our kids' reading to them before they go to bed. My kids enjoy that time with her so much and I try to do it more as well.

When we read it helps in their development. They learn new words and concepts, plus it fosters creativity. During or after I read them stories their little wheels are turning and they start asking questions and creating stories themselves.

Be creative when you read by acting out the story and read it how you think the character would sound. It is ok to be silly about it too. I like to get my British accent out or try to sound like the characters as much as I can. This makes it fun and keeps the kids engaged in the story.

21. Surprise Them

We all enjoy a good surprise once in a while. The surprises that bring joy to our life. Part of being a fun dad is being spontaneous and surprising our children with special gifts and fun things to do.

We may go to a donut shop before school, get ice cream after school, or I will put an encouraging note in their lunchbox. On the last day of school last year my wife and I surprised our kids with a trip to Chicago full of fun sites and activities. Spur of the moment picnics or getaways are always fun.

When your children are behaving well and doing well in school, reward them with a special surprise. If they are going through a tough time, a fun surprise may be exactly what they needed to lift their spirits. These fun surprises are great rewards, spirit lifters, and just one more way to show our children how much we care about them.

22. 3,2,1...Blast Off!

My son loves rockets. When he was at a wishing well getting ready to throw his penny in to make a wish I heard him say "I wish I had rockets". He talks non-stop about rockets. He draws them, acts like he has them on his bicycle, and had been pushing me to build one. One day I decided to build one with him. I had him draw out his rocket design and we gathered up all these random items to build one. We built it in about an hour and he was so proud of it. It was so fun working on it together and I even kept his little blueprints.

My kids and I have built stuff for school, made indoor tents, snow forts, and other cool things. We have fun doing it and the kids learn from these relationship building moments. They learn about tool uses, safety, and how to assemble things. The feeling they get from the accomplishment of building something is the greatest reward.

Get in the Game

To "get in the game" means to be an involved father. Before we dive in, I want to highlight some stats I found around father involvement.

46% of fathers feel they spend too little time with their children.

Source: March 14, 2013 Pew Research Center Report: "Modern Parenthood: Roles of Moms and Dads Converge as They Balance Work and Family"

49% of working fathers missed a significant event in their child's life due to work at least once in the last year and nearly one in five (18%) have missed four or more.

Source: 2007 Survey by Careerbuilder.com, from www.Fathers.com/statistics-and-research/trendsinfathering 10/26/2015

We are going to miss out on things, but we have to make every effort to be involved. Our involvement will have positive impact on our kids, academically, emotionally, and behaviorally. Let's talk about ways to get involved.

23. Be Engaged

I have always taken my professional career very seriously and invested so much of my time to be successful. One thing I have always made sure is that I am an engaged father. I try to be active in all facets of their life.

I have not been to every event they had, and I never will be. I try to be at 90+% of them and I make every effort to do so. When we become fully engaged in their lives it shows them we care.

Our involvement shows our children they can count on us to be there, it creates memories, and it carries through their life when they become a parent. As mentioned early, I feel it helps them emotionally, behaviorally, and academically. No matter how busy your professional life is, try to make every effort possible to be engaged in all areas of their life.

24. "Smart" TV

I will go ahead and say it, today's movie and television entertainment has really become terrible. If you look at some of the cartoon shows out there they are so inappropriate and gross. I actually felt dumber after watching a couple of these with my kids. Needless to say, we try to ban that trash.

In today's hectic world, it is too easy to let kids camp in front of a television and let it be your virtual babysitter, or to let your kid plant their face in a tablet device. If you do not pay attention, they could be watching one of those dumbing down shows out there.

The older I get the more I enjoy and appreciate good classic movies and television shows. The Andy Griffith Show is one of them. It had good messages, good humor, and reruns are on TV all the time, plus it is on Netflix. Disney also does a great job, with providing good kids programming. Actually, with the small funding it has, PBS provides some of the best content for kids. Their shows are educational, entertaining, and kid appropriate.

I know it is difficult to know everything they are watching, but I would suggest keeping close tabs on the content they view. Another area to really watch is on YouTube, where they can get exposed to a lot of bad content. You can turn the restricted mode on to filter most inappropriate content. Similar to Netflix and other content providers, look for ways to make sure your kids only have access to age-appropriate shows.

Even with these filters in place, they can still view those dumbing down shows I mentioned. When you know those are shows they like, just make it a rule with them that they are not allowed to view those programs.

With a few clicks and a few rules, you can help make sure your children minimize their exposure to programs that can be negative influences in their life.

25. Get To Know Their Friends

Our kids spend up to one-third of their childhood time surrounded by their friends. Most of that time is during school, after school playing, and other extracurricular activities. The social pressures we had growing up still exist today. I would argue those pressures are increasing.

We want to make sure we know who our kids are spending their time with and make sure those kids are good influences in their lives. When we know who they are hanging out with then we get a better understanding of how they are being influenced. We will have a better understanding if and when we should step in to diffuse any problematic behaviors or actions before they start.

I also believe that there is an extra level of respect that you may receive from their friends. Hopefully your child is respected more from their friends when they get to know you and know what you stand for.

We cannot be with our kids 24/7, but when we know who they are hanging out with then we will have a better handle on who is influencing them and the type of environment our children are subject to.

26. Coach

If you are a sports nut like me, this one is kind of an easy one. However, coaching can be a little intimidating and stressful, especially if you have never coached before or you are coaching a sport you know little or nothing about. I encourage you to try and coach when they are young even if you do not know the sport very well.

Coaching is just another way to be more directly involved in your child's life. I realize work schedules make it difficult to make this type of commitment, but from my experience most employers are accommodating. Plus, many will respect your desire to be involved in your child's sports activities.

Last year there was a sport one of my children played that I knew nothing about. I would take them to practice, do my work on the sidelines, and we would leave afterwards. Sure I would practice with them at home, but it was not until I decided the following season to help coach. I got to be more involved at practice, during the games, and at home we would strategize and practice together more.

In the past year I have helped coach five of their sports teams and I have loved every minute of it. Your children will appreciate your involvement (may take a few years for them to realize this) and this gives you some definite photo advantages!

27. Ivy League, State, or Community?

You will be touring college campuses before you know it, so make sure you invest early on. Set a goal to have most of their college costs taken care of by the time they enroll. College costs are increasing and here are average yearly costs at the different types of colleges:

Type of College	Average Published Yearly Tuition and Fees
Public Two-Year College (in-district students)	$3,347
Public Four-Year College (in-state students)	$9,139
Public Four-Year College (out-of-state students)	$22,958
Private Four-Year College	$31,231

Source: BigFuture.CollegeBoard.Org 1/19/16

I am an investor, so naturally investing in my children's college future is an area I focused on early on. Actually, when we had our first child they had a 529 Plan when they were born. I learned a lot from my father too. He set aside money every other pay check during my adolescent years, to help when it came time for me to go to college.

You can put your money in any type of investment vehicle, but the most popular one for college tuition is the 529 plan. Each state has one and you may qualify for tax benefits. Our 529 plans are structured to where I have a set amount deposited each month.

Getting involved from a financial perspective is investing in our children's future. Before you know it you will have saved a substantial amount of money to help cover the continually rising tuition costs.

28. Listen Up

It is easy for a parent to control a conversation with our children because we may think we know more due to our age and experience. Sometimes the best thing we can do is just let our children talk. Give them the mic to let them get out whatever is on their mind. They may be completely wrong on a particular viewpoint, but let them explain. When they are finished help correct them, if correcting is necessary. If they are telling a story, let them share it with you and you show interest in their creative mind sharing.

As we become older we realize that things we stressed out as children were such minor things, but at that moment they were big things to us. When your kid is stressed about something let them know you are always there for them to talk about any issue on their mind. It is important for our children to know we are there to listen to them when they need to get something off their mind.

29. Be Adventurous

I seem to become more adventurous each day. I like to try new things and visit new places. With this sense of adventure I seek ways to be inspired and for it to be a learning experience.

When our family made our first big move to another city we started saying "Let's go on an adventure". We would explore the city and see what God placed around us to experience and enjoy. As our first full summer arrived, we called it the "Summer of Adventures". The next summer we continued this journey of exploration.

The best thing about going on adventures is that we are exploring new territory…together as a family. Plus, it gives us exercise, builds excitement in seeing or doing something new, creates great memories, and we learn from many of these experiences. I also feel that it helps build confidence within our children.

Every Day Is a Classroom

Each day is like a classroom and as fathers we are teachers. We have the responsibility to share our knowledge and to help them understand. As we build on ways to be more involved, teaching takes it to the next level when we seize those opportunities to help them learn. We can approach those teaching moments in a fun-loving way, and sometimes these moments require a more serious approach to make sure they understand more effectively.

When we teach them new skills, how to do things, or how to handle situations we are setting them up for success in the future. These teaching moments can keep them safe, give them confidence by knowing how to do things, and they can shape their character as a person.

"Train a child in the way that he should go, and when he is old he will not turn from it."

– Proverbs 22:6

30. The Edison Mindset

You do not have to be an inventor, artist, or entrepreneur to be creative. It is something we all possess and it is important for us to make sure it is nurtured in our kids. We want to help foster their creative ideas by helping them unleash them by being courageous and exploring those ideas.

I am not suggesting we turn them into little Thomas Edisons (although that would be cool). Just support them in idea exploration, believe in them and give them the tools to try out their ideas.

Be open-minded and do not hinder their creativity by saying "that won't work". Living in the United States we are blessed by being in the nexus of innovation and entrepreneurialism. Supporting our children in their ideas helps them understand that failure is a possibility, but perseverance and never giving up is what makes one successful.

31. Set An Example

The best Earthly role model a kid can have is their parent. We are given many opportunities in life to set an example for our kids. Take advantage of those times in order for our kids to learn from us.

Many of the opportunities I come across are in the area of helping others in need. It could be a person needing money, someone needing help doing something, or donating something to someone.

When our children observe us doing a genuine act of kindness it makes them want to do it in the future. I have seen that first hand with my kids. There have been many times where they helped someone with something, or they wanted to give money to an organization to help others. Seeing their kind hearts makes you very proud as a parent and it also makes you feel like you are doing something right as a parent.

Today's generation of children need good role models. Role models that display acts of kindness, love, compassion, and a willingness to offer up something to someone else without expecting anything in return. When you see those opportunities seize them! Set that example for your child.

"In everything set them an example by doing what is good. In your teaching show integrity..."
- Titus 2:7

32. Always Watching

I have often heard people say children are like little sponges in that they absorb so much around them. I think a better example is they are like little spy cameras, watching and listening to everything we do. Have you ever heard your child say an inappropriate word or do a not so pleasant action? If you ask them where they learned that they may have said "from you Dad".

As an adult we have the freedom to say and do many things, but some of them are things not to be passed down. The first example that comes to mind is cursing. I have done it, but it is still wrong. I have also vented to my wife about something and the kids hear it. They then think it is ok to not like what I was venting about. We need to take those venting sessions offline and not in the kids presence. Watching what we say and do applies to others things, such as driving, boasting, how we treat others, or any other inappropriate habits.

The point is if it is something we do not want our kids saying or doing then we should watch what we do or say in front of them. Chances are it is probably something we should not be saying or doing anyway. As Barney Fife always said, "Nip it in the bud".

"Do not let any unwholesome talk come out of your mouths, but only what is helpful for building others up according to their needs, that it may benefit those who listen."

– Ephesians 4:29

33. Being a Good Husband

I am in no means the perfect husband, but I always try to be a good husband. I tell my wife I love her all the time, I show her respect, I listen to her (most of the time), and I do my best to support her in any way I can. If we can be good husbands, then especially if you have a son, they will take note of how we should show love and respect to our wife.

Maybe you are in a situation where you and the mother are not married. You can still show the same traits of being supportive, listening, and showing respect to her. Our children observe those interactions and as a man we need to always treat a woman with respect.

> "Husbands, love your wives, just as Christ loved the church and gave himself up for her…"
> – Ephesians 5:25

34. Mission: Safe Kid

There is a new parental term I got introduced to last year and it was called a "helicopter" parent. I would not necessarily call myself one of those, but I have had a few chopper pilot moments. From my childhood I was always a worrier and after given the responsibility of having children I worry even more, particularly about their safety.

The world is much more dangerous now than it was when I was growing up. When I reflect back on my childhood I thank God for having several guardian angels following me and keeping me safe. We will not always be able to keep our kids safe, but there are steps we can take to help keep them safer.

- Teach them your phone numbers: home, cell, work, and when to use 911. If they are too young make sure they are listed on a backpack or somewhere they know where to find them.

- Do online neighborhood criminal watch search. You can view your neighborhood to see if any criminals live nearby. Also check near your kid's school, or near locations your child visits.

- Make sure your children know what to do when approached by a stranger.

- Teach them how to avoid, resist, and escape violence or harm to their lives.

- Explain how to respond to and avoid bullying.

- Teach fire safety and what to do in case of natural disasters. Fire and police departments, and the Red Cross are places to inquire about seminars to help in emergency preparedness.

These are just a few steps to help create a safer environment for your child. It is important to pray every day to God that your children are safe and that they make good decisions to stay out of harm's way.

"God is our refuge and strength, an ever-present help in trouble."

– **Psalm 46:1**

35. Saving Money

This will be one of the most important things you can teach your children at a young age. Today's younger generations have a sense of entitlement and live in the "I want it now" mindset. Unfortunately, most of our schools are not teaching the importance of saving and investing either, so we must teach them at home and instill this knowledge and behavior at an early age.
We all know that saving our money and making good investment choices are key to achieving financial goals. If our children are not going to learn key financial principles in school then we need to take the lead as parents to teach them.

If they see you wasting your money or drowning in debt then there is a good chance they may pick up your money management behaviors. We need to prevent that, so you need to be a good steward of your own money first. There are so many great resources out there to learn from…..online seminars, local classes at libraries and non-profits, and a ton of books around getting out of debt, budgeting, financial planning, saving, and more. So many people are struggling financially and that is why I published a book called "A Money Saving Mindset" to help people save their hard earned money. It has changed the lives of so many people and led them to a path of better financial stewardship.

So let's say you have your financial house in order…good! Now you need to share your knowledge with your kids. Give them real life examples of how you saved up to buy something (ex: pay for college, buy a car, purchase a home) and help them understand by saving their allowance or gift money, (or paycheck if they are working) to purchase one of their wants (ex: a new toy, car, gift for someone). When they earn or receive money have them get in the habit of saving a large portion of it. They will be surprised to see how quickly it adds up!

For an extra step, talk to them about investing too. Investing is also important as it helps them understand putting their money to work for them so they can accumulate more. When I was in fifth grade I had my first shares of stock. I was kind of geeky in that for my whole childhood I would read all the ticker symbols and stock prices in the newspaper. Many years later, my passion for researching stocks still exists. I can say what my dad and uncle Bill taught me early on in saving and investing has helped me get to where I am today.

36. Learning From You

Kids are eager to learn and love to be included in things. Especially if they can participate in something that makes them feel bigger. Many of the skills we teach them will stick with them and help them later in life. I am in my 40's and I am still learning things from my dad. Over these 40 some years so many of the things I have had to do I learned from my dad (and mom too!).

So what are some of the things you could teach your kid to do? Well of course it depends on their age, but even if they could just watch and sit with you they are learning and you are building that relationship. You can have them help you work on simple, safe things around the house. When we work on something I always make them wear safety glasses, and usually gloves. That instantly makes them feel involved.

If you have something that is too difficult for them to do, you can still put them in a safe setting and allow them to help you. It could be to help hold the flashlight for you while you work on plumbing under the sink, they can hand you tools while you are working on your car, or just simply talk to each other and enjoy that time together.

Use these moments to teach them new skills, teach safety, and explain the types of tools & terminology. These opportunities will give them responsibility, build your relationships, and give them lifelong skills.

37. Bring Back Chivalry

Chivalry is when a man is polite and displays a kind behavior that shows respect to a woman. I will add that we show this to <u>every</u> woman. Not just a wife, mother, or friend, but being chivalrous to a stranger. In our fast paced society, chivalry is becoming a lost trait. I have even heard some people say that chivalry is dead.

We can show chivalry in a variety of ways. You can simply open the door for someone, give up your seat for a woman, offer a woman to go ahead of you in line, or carry something for them. If you travel, offer to help assist a woman put her luggage in the airplane overhead.

There are many ways to show chivalry and they are so simple. When your children see you do this then they are more likely to do the same. If every man did this simple act just once a day, we could change the world before our eyes.

38. Respect

When I was growing up my dad said the most important attribute I could have was earning the respect of others. He also said that respect is something that takes time to build and once you earn that respect it can open doors and create opportunities for you. Respect is also something that you can lose very quickly based on a stupid decision that you make. I have always applied those teachings to my daily life.

With every interaction I have with someone I work hard to show my respect to them as well as hope to earn their respect for me. I believe it says something about your character too. There are many people I talk to who want to own the conversation, be a know it all, or always try to one up you. Needless to say, I struggle with respecting that person very much because of that character trait they have. When I leave an interaction, I want to have in my mind that I did the best I could in having them leave with a good impression and with respect for me.

Earning respect is not only by the words we speak, but also through our actions. We gauge people on our respect meters in how someone acts at a social event, ballgame, what they post on social media, etc. Think about this....are you going to hire someone you do not respect? Are you going to go out of your way to help out someone low on your respect meter? You might or might not. We tend to go out of our way for people we respect.

We need to work hard to earn the respect of everyone, and try to make sure our children model respectful behaviors as well.

39. Integrity

Someone who has integrity is someone who is honest and adheres to moral and ethical principles. In my fifteen years in the corporate world, integrity was an area we were measured on for performance reviews. Unfortunately, integrity is lacking throughout the corporate world.

Integrity ties closely to the respect section we covered. If you have strong moral character and can be trusted, then having integrity is the key component for earning the respect of others. Like respect, it takes time to build an integrity reputation. Through your actions you can display integrity to others, and with that respect is earned.

If you strive to achieve and maintain integrity in everything you do your children will notice. Look for ways to reinforce being a person of integrity to your children through the choices they make.

Make integrity be a goal of you and your children's reputation as it will always be a way of how we are measured, through career performance reviews or how well people trust and respect us.

"The righteous man leads a blameless life; blessed are his children after him."
– Proverbs 20:7

40. Gratitude

It always feels nice when you do something for someone and they tell you "thanks". I do not ever expect a favor in return, but the simple acknowledgement of a thank you is appreciated. When someone does something for me I try to always thank them.

We are becoming a world that is busier and busier by the minute. We have so many things competing for our mindshare and we are getting closer to system overload. I think another change is society is becoming more of a "me" society.

Regardless of how busy our lives are we all have a second to spare to show our gratitude to others. When we show gratitude our children pick up on that and are likely to replicate that behavior.

Gratitude goes beyond just saying thanks all the time. You can do something nice in return for someone, send them a card, or give them a gift. Showing your appreciation will go a long way. People will remember your gracious efforts. Remember to every day give thanks to Jesus Christ!

> "...give thanks in all circumstances, for this is God's will for you in Christ Jesus."
> – 1 Thessalonians 5:18

Ready to Be a Next Level Dad?

Throughout this book I have given you many things to think about incorporating into your role as a father. I am sure you are doing some of them and I hope that there are many new ideas to start doing now. There are more ways, but these are some of my favorite ways of taking being a father to the next level.

When I think about the blessing and responsibility that God gave me of being a father I take it seriously and I do not take it for granted. My goal as a father is pretty simple:

1) Help my kids grow closer in their relationship with Jesus Christ – by praying, studying the Bible, serving and caring for others, and worshipping Jesus.

2) Help them build a foundation of fatherly wisdom. Strive to find those teachable moments that will help them in life.

3) To be a fun dad who is full of adventure. Having a sense of humor, making them laugh, and looking for ways to help them learn and experience the world around them.

4) Always be there for them. By being involved in all facets of their life, by listening to them, and having them know they can always come to me for anything.

Our children will be grown up before we know it. We will be looking back wondering where the time went and asking ourselves; "Did I do a good job as a father?" When I think about my own legacy there are so many things I hope my children will have learned from me and be prepared for in the world ahead. This book and others I write are small ways I hope to contribute and make an impact.

Of all the things we hope to pass down to them and they carry with them into their life, the most important item is that they understand the importance of having a relationship with Jesus Christ. I hope my kids see from me that I was a man of God, who had a strong faith, and believed so much in the importance of prayer. I am in no means perfect, but I try to live my life in a Christ-like manner. I can only hope that they will model themselves after Jesus.

"Show me your ways, O Lord, teach me your paths; guide me in your truth and teach me, for you are God my Savior, and my hope is in you all day long."

– Psalm 25:4-5

A Prayer for You

I pray that God will bless you with the wisdom you need to guide you through all areas of your father role. I pray that you will always seek God's help through daily prayer. I also pray that you will strive to be the best father you can be, by encouraging, supporting, teaching, and loving your children. Jesus Christ is the best role model any of us can have and I pray that the Lord will help you lead and father in a Christ-like manner.

I like to share my faith ever since I put my trust in Jesus Christ in March 2003. The decision I made to follow Christ has changed my life. It has made me a better, stronger man. It has also made me a better husband and a better father.

If you have never committed your life to following Christ and want God's gift of eternal life, it starts with a simple prayer:

"Dear Heavenly Father, I know I am a sinner. Please forgive me of my sins. I believe you sent Jesus Christ down to this earth to live a sinless life. He made the ultimate sacrifice by dying on the cross and rose from the dead, all so we could be forgiven of our sins and have eternal life in Heaven. From this day forward, I accept Jesus Christ as my personal Lord and Savior."

If you said this prayer and invited Jesus Christ into your heart, you have just made the best decision of your life! Your next step is to just reach out to a local pastor and they will guide you on the next steps of your new Christian life.

About the Author

Derek is a married father of two kids. Having a passion for the business world, Derek obtained business degrees at Vincennes University and Indiana State University.

A lifelong learner and while he and his wife were expecting their first child, Derek achieved an MBA from the University of Southern Indiana. He also completed professional development programs from Duke, Harvard, M.I.T., and Northwestern. His professional experience includes roles in Product Management and Supply Chain Management.

He likes to go on adventures with his family, invest in stocks, watch movies, and follow his favorite sports teams. Derek is a follower of Jesus Christ and forever thankful to his personal Savior.

Read Derek's Other Popular Book:

A Money Saving Mindset:
40 Ways to Help You Save

www.AMoneySavingMindset.com

Available at Amazon or BN.com

Sources:

Scripture taken from the HOLY BIBLE, NEW INTERNATIONAL VERSION ®, Copyright © 1973, 1978, 1984 by International Bible Society. Used by permission of Zondervan Publishing House. All rights reserved.